How to create effective information and communication technology learning programmes

a guide

NIACE
THE NATIONAL ORGANISATION
FOR ADULT LEARNING

How to create effective information and communication technology learning programmes

a guide

Alan Clarke

Published by the National Institute of
Adult Continuing Education (England and Wales)

21 De Montfort Street
Leicester LE1 7GE
Company registration no. 2603322
Charity registration no. 1002775

First published 1999

NIACE, the national organisation for adult learning,
has a broad remit to promote lifelong learning
opportunities for adults. NIACE works to develop
increased participation in education and training,
particularly for those who do not have easy access
because of barriers of class, gender, age, race,
language and culture, learning difficulties and
disabilities, or insufficient financial resources.

NIACE's website on the Internet is http://www.niace.org.uk

Cataloguing in Publication Data
A CIP record of this title is available from the British Library

Designed and typeset by Boldface
Printed in Great Britain by Russell Press, Nottingham

ISBN 1 86201 054 4

Contents

Acknowledgements

I would like to thank the Training Technology Unit of the Department for Education and Employment for their permission to reproduce some of the outcomes of *IT Awareness for Adults* (Clarke, 1998) in this guide. Also Jackie Essom for her careful proof-reading of the drafts and the many IT tutors who shared their experiences with me.

The ICT examples in this guide are based on Windows 95 operating system.

Computer hardware and software brand names mentioned in this guide are protected by their respective trade marks and are acknowledged.

Introduction

For many adults information technology is associated with doubt, uncertainty and a lack of confidence. It requires them to make a considerable effort simply to attend an introductory event. These fears probably spring from the perception that new technology is difficult to understand. The government's IT for All programme has identified through recent surveys that more than half the adult population are concerned, unconvinced or alienated by information technology. Only about 20 per cent of adults are confident in their understanding of information technology. The emerging information society will certainly not be an inclusive world unless there is major growth in the proportion of adults who are competent users of IT.

Adults who overcome their doubts to enrol on an initial event must be presented with an experience which encourages them to return for more. It is quite possible within a short period to provide an experience which starts the process of developing confidence, reassures the participants that they can learn about computers and encourages them to return. When learners have a satisfactory initial learning experience they will often return with a friend, their partner or a child. This clearly shows that they have been convinced that they can learn about information and communication technology and that it is important for everyone. You know you have failed to overcome these doubts and uncertainties when the learners do not return.

2 Planning a programme

WHY DO ADULTS WANT TO LEARN ABOUT ICT?

In designing any programme of learning, the learners' needs and motives for attending are the most important element. The main reasons adults give for wanting to learn about information technology (Clarke, 1998) are:

▶ to help their children or grandchildren
'I need to learn computer skills for future use with my child'

▶ the fear of being left behind
'Wanted to keep up with my eight-year old son'

▶ to make themselves more employable
'To help me with my work'

▶ simple interest and curiosity
'Interested to learn'

A series of surveys (IT for All and Microsoft) has shown that although the majority of adults have heard of personal computers and the Internet they are often in doubt about their relevance to their own lives. This is in contrast to their view that ICT is critically important to the future prosperity of the United Kingdom. It seems to suggest that adults see IT as something for other people and not themselves. It is therefore important to structure your initial and subsequent events to allow the learners to identify reasons why IT can benefit them. Some applications you might want to use to demonstrate the relevance of ICT are:

- ▶ educational multimedia products
- ▶ Internet sites relevant to learners such as hobbies (see Figure 1), shopping, and on-line newspapers
- ▶ paint applications
- ▶ desktop publishing
- ▶ word-processing
- ▶ spreadsheets
- ▶ databases.

Most new learners will have some degree of doubt about information technology. This doubt is often a mixture of whether they can learn to use it and whether it is useful to them. It is therefore important that they gain confidence quickly. The first experience must help them develop confidence. A short positive experience will convince many people to return for more. This initial experience can be as little as 30 minutes.

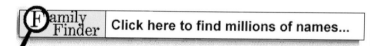

Family Finder | **Click here to find millions of names...**

Sponsored by Family Tree Maker Online

The Genealogy Home Page

Recent additions to this and related pages are shown on the What's New listing (updated frequently). More new genealogy related WWW sites can be found on the What's Really New in WWW Genealogy Pages page (updated daily).

Figure I Hobbies on the World Wide Web

(REPRODUCED WITH THE PERMISSION OF STEPHEN A. WOOD URL: http://www.genhomepage.com/)

Learners often describe themselves as complete beginners. However, their experience will vary. Some learners will never have touched a computer while others will use a computer everyday in order to carry out a narrow prescribed task without any wider understanding. Some learners will have extensive experience of a specialist word-processor but have never used other applications. They may have had a break away from computers so they feel they are beginning again. They may have bought a computer and are struggling to use it. Some will have attended a previous course but found it too difficult. In any group of beginners you may find people with similar experiences. Flexibility is likely to be important, with the learners being given a large degree of choice. However, to make an effective choice requires knowledge and understanding. So initially it may be useful to provide brief tasters of a range of applications.

Apart from their experience with ICT learners will also have different needs. It is important to be able to support and assist learners:

▶ whose first language is not English
▶ who are disabled
▶ who have learning difficulties
▶ who are visually impaired
▶ who are from different cultures

Appendix 1 provides a range of addresses of useful organisations who can provide assistance.

INDEPENDENT LEARNERS

A key aim of any information technology programme should be to develop learners who are independent. That is, learners who are able to develop their understanding independently of their tutor, learners who can cope with new releases of applications and even new applications without help and who can deal with many of the common problems of using ICT (e.g. where did I put that file? what did I call it?) without immediately seeking assistance. The pace of

ICT change is significant. Sixty per cent of ICT applications are only two years old and the shelf life of specific ICT knowledge is estimated to be only two years. Both these statistics indicate the need for learners who can cope with a rapid rate of change.

To achieve independence is not simple in a complex subject such as information technology. It is very easy to focus on helping beginners to use applications such as word-processing and omit to explain the structure of folders and directories. A great deal of initial learning is likely to concentrate on functional knowledge. That is, knowledge which tells you how to carry out a task. The example (see Figure 2) below shows you how to access the in-built calculator in Windows 95. This type of functional knowledge is required for many computing tasks. However, it is not very useful when something changes or goes wrong.

Example

Functional Knowledge – Accessing the Calculator in Windows 95

Click on Start
Select Programs – a list of applications will appear
Choose Accessories – another list of applications appear
Choose Calculator

Figure 2 Example: functional and structural understanding

In order to cope with changes or problems the learner needs to develop structural understanding. Structural knowledge allows you to predict how to do things. For example, knowing the hierarchy of the directories allows you to search through them. It allows you to guess where you are likely to find a file or where to save it to. To become an independent learner/user of information technology you require a degree of structural understanding. Without this knowledge the learner will be frequently puzzled by his or her computer and in doubt about how to do things.

A balance needs to be struck between functional and structural content. Functional knowledge tends to be associated with achieving goals (e.g. accessing a program the learner wants) and is often motivating for the learner, while structural knowledge can appear to be theoretical. However, the best approach is to combine the functional and structural aspects so that everything forms a part of an objective the learner is seeking to achieve (e.g. taking advantage of locating a program to show the hierarchy of folders).

The amount of structural underpinning a new learner needs is difficult to judge but the list below covers many important aspects which must be mastered to achieve independence. They do not all need to be learnt at once and are best integrated into a course of study lasting many weeks.

Structural

The following are examples of activities which provide a means of developing structural understanding:

- start and shut down the computer
- install software
- change system characteristics (mouse buttons, speed of double clicking, background colours and screen savers)
- mouse pointer changing shape
- create a folder and a sub-folder (understand directory structure)
- move and copy files
- delete files (single and groups of files)
- create a file
- name and rename files
- use of wild cards
- examine a folder and understand information (size of files, date created, etc.)
- format a floppy disk
- write protect disks and files
- backup files
- save files on a floppy and hard disk
- save as function
- anti-virus measures

▶ select printers
▶ print a file on a printer

One approach is to include structural items within the normal activities of introducing learners to computer systems and applications. This is a natural method which is effective as long as you do not overwhelm the learners with too much new information. Take advantage of the opportunities which present themselves. Many learners are curious about what happens inside the system and are interested in how it all fits together. This in many ways is the structural understanding which will help them to become independent ICT learners.

Examples

1. Start and shut down the computer
Switching the computer on is a fundamental skill which needs to be included in any initial course. However, it can be used to develop a wider and deeper understanding of the computer by some simple actions:

▶ Ask the learners to observe the messages which appear on the screen and explain their meaning. This allows you to explain the components of the computer as the system checks each element (e.g. CD-ROM, etc.).

▶ Ask them to listen to the sounds which the computer makes and explain that it is the hard disk searching for information. This allows you to introduce them to the nature of information storage.

▶ Ask them to observe the lights which appear on the various components. This allows you to explain some of the components of the computer (e.g. floppy disk drive).

2. Change system characteristics
A proportion of any group of learners are left-handed and will want

the mouse changed to suit their needs. This requires accessing the control panel settings which provides a wide range of opportunities to show the adaptable nature of the system:

- display resolutions
- finding files
- fonts
- add and remove hardware and software
- accessibility options

3. Save as function
Saving a file in a new location provides you with an opportunity to explore the structure of folders and files, reveal the different types of file and develop the learners understanding of how information is stored in the system.

PREPARING SESSIONS

The key to preparing for a session or a course of many sessions is basically the same. You need to think through the subject content and how best to assist the individuals to learn that subject. Preparation takes a lot of time and from scratch is likely to take approximately eight hours for each hour of a session. The process below is a general approach to preparing for a session or sessions which you may find useful to consider:

- Decide on the objectives for the session or whole programme which are suitable for students' needs and expectations, and also challenging, interesting and fun to do.
- Identify content which will help you meet your objectives. Consider alternatives, examples and context. How will you assess that the learners have achieved the objectives?
- Consider how you will present the content (e.g. exercises, hand-outs, visual aids, notes, demonstrations, individual and group activities). Develop the presentation resources.

- Break the session or programme down into meaningful parts.
- Review previous work with students especially if it relates to a new area.
- Consider how you will introduce each new area showing why it is important and providing a context for it. How will you relate it to previous work if that is relevant?
- Consider how you will work through each part. How will you allow learners to work at their own pace with plenty of opportunities to practice? How will you review individual achievements and provide individual support?
- How will you evaluate each session and the whole course? How will you obtain feedback from the students?
- How will you use the outcomes of the evaluation to influence the design of future sessions?

LOCATION

A wide range of locations have been successfully used to provide basic IT education and training. Portable equipment can establish a computer classroom in most locations (e.g. library, play scheme and village hall). Laptop computers and portable printers for a small group can be transported in an average-sized car and installation can be achieved quickly with the minimum of assistance. In common with most adult education and training the tutors first task is to move the furniture to create a good learning environment.

Any location must be acceptable to the learner. In many ways the choice of site will determine who attends. The other critical factors are the timing of the event and the distance the learners must travel to attend. An event held in a primary school starting at 9am is likely to attract the parents or grandparents of children attending the school and particularly the adult who brings the child to school. Learners are usually willing to attend a session if it is a short distance from their homes and in a familiar site.

Some simple tips for undertaking an outreach event are given overleaf:

▶ Consider the catchment area of the location. Who lives within 15 minutes' walk of the site? Who normally visits this venue? Who is likely to attend at this starting time?

▶ Consider if a crèche would be helpful.

▶ Arrive in plenty of time since you can never be sure what you will find. In particular make sure it is a safe environment for the learners. Portable equipment often means extension cables so be careful how you use them.

▶ Be flexible. Do not plan an event which depends on a certain size or shape of room.

▶ Be prepared to move the furniture to get the best layout.

▶ If you are using computers provided by the location you must check them. A school may well use software protection systems to prevent access to parts of the system which control the set-up and access to some applications (e.g. games).

▶ Take spare cables, extra equipment, fuses and anything else that might be useful.

▶ Signpost the room at least on the door.

▶ Provide some refreshments – a break is a useful way to allow learners to ask you and each other questions which they feel unable to ask in the classroom.

▶ Start and finish on time.

MARKETING

The interest in learning about ICT is very extensive so that even simple marketing devices are likely to be successful. However, it is more difficult if you want to target a specific group of learners (e.g. older learners, residents on a particular housing estate and lone parents). An effective approach is to market the places where you target group work, visit, live or go shopping. Different age groups gain their information from different sources. The workplace is important to 25- to 54-year-olds; young people gain their knowledge from more formal sources such as the careers service; and older people rely more on informal channels such as word of mouth, libraries and advertisements (Sargant *et al*, 1997).

Straightforward approaches which have proved effective are:

- ▶ Posters, e.g. in libraries, shop windows, community centres, job clubs, course site and other community locations.
- ▶ Leaflets, e.g. inserted in local free newspapers, displayed in community locations, delivered through letter boxes and are available in pubs.
- ▶ Postcards can be an attractive and cost effective means of gaining interest.
- ▶ Word of mouth is a very powerful means of marketing a course. However, it also unpredictable.

The location of your marketing is likely to have a significant impact on who attends your courses. It is important to consider before you start what are the likely effects of marketing in a particular place.

A free event will attract a large number of learners. However, if charging is introduced later the obvious happens in that numbers will be dramatically reduced.

TASTERS

A taster is intended to provide a learner with an opportunity to experience ICT in some way. It could be to see and use the Internet or to work through a computer-based learning package or try out a multimedia product. To achieve the best results a taster should be more than a demonstration. It should encourage learners to have a go and ideally allow them to achieve a goal they can identify with. It is important that they have some choice and individuals will often request the opportunity to try a particular product. However, the majority of beginners will not have sufficient knowledge of ICT to make an informed choice and will need the tutor's guidance. Both the Government's IT for All programme and the BBC's Computers Don't Bite campaign have developed taster materials in the form of multimedia CD-ROMs. These provide an intro-duction to ICT for the new learner which is both effective and allows them a degree of choice.

A short taster event is often very popular and effective in overcoming learners' anxieties and doubts about learning about ICT. Taster sessions are highly flexible and combined with portable computers can take the experience to a wide range of target groups.

Events have been successfully provided at many locations including a holiday play scheme, supermarkets, pubs, workplaces, community centres, schools and libraries.

A good taster event is:

▶ Short (approximately an hour or less) and easy to combine with other activities (e.g. a visit to the library, attending a play scheme or going shopping).
▶ Practical and hands-on. It is not enough to demonstrate ICT – learners need the opportunity to use it.
▶ Free. This removes a major barrier and persuades learners who are visiting the location for other reasons to have a go.
▶ Non-threatening and fun.
▶ Structured so that learners will successfully use ICT.
▶ Offered in an acceptable location.

Taster sessions have been found to be an effective approach to motivating adults to seek further education and training. A taster event is an effective means of recruiting for longer ICT courses of study. Many adults will commit themselves to a course following a successful taster event.

DROP-IN CENTRES

Drop-in centres are a popular and effective means of providing access to ICT. They can take many forms from the small temporary site established in a community location to a permanent learning centre with a wide range of sophisticated applications and equipment. Centres serve a number of different purposes:

▶ The temporary centre is often intended to provide a basic introduction, raise awareness or offer a series of tasters. Drop-in services can be quite small and operate from what would seem to be inappropriate locations due to background noise or other distractions. They can almost be considered as a marketing exercise recruiting learners for conventional courses. In order to succeed the provision needs to be integrated into other appropriate learning opportunities. Centres often develop regular customers who can block access for new learners if there are not clear progression routes.

▶ Permanent centres are often seen as cost-effective ways of providing ICT learning when combined with good quality open learning materials. The key to success is sufficient timely support for the learner. A tutor is likely to find supporting a busy drop-in facility demanding in that she or he will often be working with individuals across a wide range of abilities and interests without a pause.

Learners often identified two factors which make them unwilling to continue to use a centre. These are:

▶ waiting for support; and
▶ frequent changes in tutor support.

Learners need to have their questions answered promptly and be able to develop a relationship with the tutor.

HEALTH AND SAFETY

Most adults who attend an initial ICT event will be new to computers. They are therefore unaware of the risks involved (e.g. repetitive strain injury). It is therefore critical to provide a safe and healthy environment for them to learn in.

An outreach or temporary site needs to be considered prior to the first course and rejected if it is not a safe environment in which to learn. Once you have assessed the centre's hazards you must remove them.

There is a range of straightforward measures which you can take in organising the physical structure of the room and the session which can contribute to a safe learning environment. The main points are:

Individual space

Each learner should be comfortable, with sufficient space to be able to reach and see both the computer and their learning materials without having to twist and turn too much. Learners have to layout their exercises and handouts so individual workspace needs to allow for their materials. The position of the computer screen and input devices should be adjusted to suit the individual needs of the learner. Learners with special needs should be consulted to ensure that the facilities are suitable.

Seating

Seats should be adjustable and learners should be shown how to adjust the height and backrest to ensure they are comfortable. The learners lower back needs to be supported by the chair and feet should be able to be placed flat on the floor or on a footrest.

The height of the chair should allow the learner's eyes to be aligned slightly below the top of the screen.

Height of equipment

For wheelchair users it is important that the computer system is positioned at a suitable height so they are able to use the keyboard and mouse without difficulty.

Typing

There are some simple tips to avoiding placing strain on hands and wrists. They are:

▶ Keep wrists straight while typing.

- Keep forearms horizontal.
- Adjust the keyboard to reduce strain.
- Avoid resting on wrists (be careful that in temporary locations your tables are not too small so that wrists and arms are not supported by the desk).
- Type gently and the strain is reduced. There is no need to pound the keys to enter text.
- Learners should not be allowed to type for long periods without a break. Keep exercises short and integrate frequent breaks into the structure of the session.

Light

Try to position screens so they do not reflect light from the sun or artificial lights. Each learner should individually adjust brightness and contrast of the monitor to meet their needs. This is also a good way of starting to break down any barriers or fears about computers which the individuals may have.

Food and drink

Food and drink do not mix with computers. Refreshment breaks should be taken away from the computers.

Wires

A common problem is trailing cables and it is important to remove them so that the risk is eliminated. If you need to use extension leads, then place them under furniture in such a way that it is impossible to trip and fall over them.

Fire

In any location you are working in it is your responsibility to ensure that the learners know what to do in the event of a fire. You should explain the fire procedure at the start of the event.

3 Opening session of an ICT programme

THE INITIAL EXPERIENCE

The first experience of computers needs to concentrate on the development of the learners' confidence. It must be a motivating experience so that they are encouraged to learn more. Some possible tasks which have been successfully used to break the ice are:

▶ using Computers Don't Bite or IT for All introductory CD-ROMs
▶ playing a game (e.g. Solitaire)
▶ searching a database for information
▶ using a multimedia encyclopaedia
▶ producing an electronic picture
▶ shopping on the World Wide Web
▶ doing a quiz.

The initial session needs to focus on building confidence. It is important to:

▶ give encouragement
▶ avoid jargon
▶ reduce anxiety
▶ provide clear and concise handouts
▶ encourage mutual support
▶ explain what their options are (e.g. longer course, drop-in centre, etc.).

LEARNING STYLES

People learn in different ways. There is no perfect approach to learning which suits everyone. One way of considering how individuals learn has been called learning preferences or styles. Each individual has preferences which are called her or his learning style. These are each individual's normal approaches to learning. Individuals are normally unaware that they have preferences. They will often tell you that they find learning in certain situations difficult. This may be due to the teaching approach and not relating to their learning style. Frequently individuals identify the problem as their own failure. One way of categorising learning styles is presented as two intersecting continuum (see Figure 3). These are Verbal-Imagery and Holist-Analytical. These different elements reflect how individuals deal with information and how they prefer it to be presented to them.

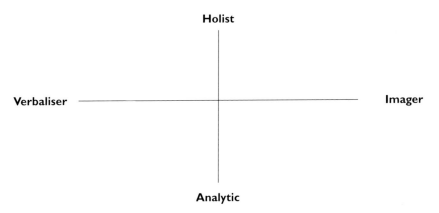

Figure 3 Verbal-Imagery and Holist-Analytical dimensions

The characteristics of the different factors are:

Holist-Analytic (Figure 4)

Holists see information as a whole. They have an overall view of the situation in its context and find it difficult to see any separate parts. In fact, as far as a holist is concerned there are no individual parts. In a learning situation a holist would have difficulty identifying individual components but no problems gaining a balanced view.

Holist   **Analytic**

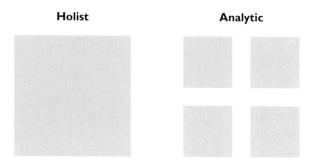

Figure 4 Holist-Analytic

Analytical individuals will consider each part separately and this may cause them to exaggerate the importance of individual aspects out of context with the whole. However, they can analyse information which often allows them to quickly see the issues. They are effective at comparing and contrasting the different components.

In a learning environment holists need help in seeing the component parts while analytics will find discerning the whole difficult. In a computer context a holist will be able to perceive the different elements which make up a computer as one system. However, they may have more difficulty in appreciating the role of each part.

Verbalisers-Imagers

This dimension represents the way individuals think about the information being presented to them and how they prefer information to be presented to them. Verbalisers prefer to consider information as words while imagers consider information as a mental picture. There are also many individuals who can use either way of representing information.

In a learning situation verbalisers may be at a disadvantage in a situation which presents information entirely as images. Imagers equally would be uncomfortable with information presented only as words. Both groups can change their way of considering information but it probably requires them to make an extra effort.

Individuals are a mixture of both dimensions so we have individuals who are:

▶ Holist-Verbalisers
▶ Holist-Imagers
▶ Analytic-Verbalisers
▶ Analytic-Imagers

The degree of emphasis varies between the two dimensions. In any group of learners it is not practicable to know which styles people prefer but you can be sure that each person has a different balance of styles.

This analysis leads you to providing sessions which use a range of methods to explain concepts and present information.

Examples

1. Explanation of both whole issues and their component parts.
2. Words and pictures used to illustrate points.
3. The same points explained in different ways.
4. Awareness that an individual's difficulties may relate to tutoring approach.
5. Opportunities to explore and try out learners' ideas.
6. Balance of activities – reading, listening, doing, discussing, reflecting, etc.

PARTICIPATION

Mutual support

A key resource in any classroom is the other learners. Most people are willing to help their peers. The tutor will find supporting a group of learners very demanding and there is a risk that some may have to wait too long for assistance. This can be reduced partially by encouraging learners to help each other. Equally important is that some learners will be reluctant to ask for help from the tutor but will be comfortable with a fellow learner.

Some ways to encourage communication between learners are:

▶ start the session or course with introductions so that everyone gets use to contributing
▶ learners should be seated so that it easy to co-operate with each other
▶ employ methods such as small group work, discussion groups and reviewing the course
▶ learners should be encouraged to move around the room so that they come into contact with each other and have something to discuss (e.g. examples of equipment to see and touch and new exercises and materials to collect)
▶ regular breaks to allow an opportunity to meet other learners.

Group contributions

One-to-one support is very valuable. Equally useful is the development of a group contribution or learners-to-tutor communications. This allows you to identify issues from the whole group and to change the content or approach to more closely meet the needs of the group.

Some ways to encourage group communication are:

▶ review previous session by asking the group if everything was clear or if they had any questions or comments to make

▶ discussion of subject
  ● divide into small groups and ask them to discuss a selected topic – this will help quiet students take part and ensure more whole-class debate
  ● provide them with a paper outlining the issues for discussion
  ● ask students to write down main points they want to raise before discussion begins
▶ small groups
  ● divide into small groups (two or three people) and ask them to work together to achieve an objective (e.g. to design an advertising leaflet for the course)
▶ ask questions of the whole group or individuals as you walk around the room
▶ encourage the learners to ask you questions by making yourself available and approachable.

CONTENT

There are many ways of presenting content. For new computer users the most valuable way is probably to use the equipment. They have no actual experience on which to relate any explanation you provide, so it is critically important that they are directly able to see and experience hardware and software.

Many computer concepts are very new to beginners. It is very useful to explain concepts by making comparisons with familiar objects or by using analogies. Analogies are powerful devices in that they help learners to relate the new ideas to previous experiences. Some widely used analogies are:

▶ CPU – engine in a car or the brain of the system
▶ Internet – shopping mall
▶ computer clock speed – engine capacity/size.

The language of computers has many terms which will be new to learners. These are often outside of their own experience. For example:

- CD-ROM
- floppy disk
- drive
- chip
- application
- hardware and software.

Learners often feel vulnerable and anxious because they do not know the meaning of this language. It is therefore good practice not to introduce a new term without explaining clearly its meaning. For hardware and software the learner should be given the opportunity to see, touch and use the equipment or application. For other terms a clear explanation should be given in plain English if this is possible. In addition a glossary should be provided. It is very difficult to avoid using jargon since in many cases there are no plain English equivalents (e.g. Applet) but you can explain.

In the first session the major issue for the beginner is using the two main input devices:

- keyboard
- mouse.

These devices are vital to allow the learner to interact with the system and explore this new world. Windows 95 provides options to improve accessibility for users who might find the standard settings a barrier:

- The mouse can be set for either right- or left-handed users. Some left-handed people will still prefer to use the mouse right-handed. Ask them what they want to do.
- Slow down double-clicking.
- Mouse trails to help learners find their way.
- System ignores repeated key presses.
- Sounds when capitals, number and scroll lock keys are pressed.

▶ Visual warnings when system makes a sound.
▶ Improve contrast to aid legibility.
▶ Use number pad arrow keys as an alternative to a mouse.

The use of the number pad as an alternative to the mouse is very useful to disabled learners who cannot use a mouse. However, the learner should be the person who decides whether to use a mouse or the keyboard alternative. Many disabled users have developed their own ways of using a mouse effectively including two-handed use. Figure 5 shows how to locate the accessibility options.

Accessibility Options

Windows 95 provides a number of options to help users who are disabled.

> **Click on Start button**
> **Select Settings**
> **Select Control panel**
> **Select Accessibility icon**

There are a variety of features which you choose from relating to keyboard, sound, display, mouse and general. One of the most useful functions is to replace the mouse with the numbers keys.

Explore these options.

Figure 5 Accessibility options

The content of the first session depends on the needs of the learners. Four approaches are given below depending on the motivation of the learner:

1. Never touched a computer

Explain the component parts of the system in simple terms:
▶ monitor
▶ CPU

- keyboard
- mouse
- CD-ROM drive (show them a CD-ROM disk)
- floppy drive (show them a floppy disk).

Using a mouse
- how to hold a mouse
  - for a right-handed user
  - for a left-handed user
- how to move a mouse
- what do different buttons do?
- clicking – remember differences between left- and right-handed users
  - single-clicking
  - double-clicking (remember learners find speed of double-clicking difficult and this needs to be emphasised)
  - clicking and dragging
- changing shape of pointer
  - arrow
  - flashing bar
  - hour glass
  - cross
  - arrow and hour glass

Using a keyboard
- simple overview of a QWERTY keyboard showing layout
  - number keys
  - function keys
  - alphabetical keys
  - shift key linked to upper case letters
  - backspace to delete
  - enter key
  - space bar

Learners should be provided with one or two exercises to practise inserting letters and spaces, etc.
- entering and editing text
  - ask learners to type in some text (e.g. own name, etc.)

- edit some words already entered (e.g. deleting letters, inserting text, etc.)
- explain and show pointer changing shape from arrow, to I bar to flashing bar
- positioning of cursor in the middle of words

2. Use a computer at work but don't understand what it is all about

The first step is to find out what they do. Computers are used in a wide variety of tasks and functions. If they are skilled keyboard and mouse users then there is little point in getting them to practise these skills, so introduce them to new challenges. Often people who spend their working days inputting data have little knowledge outside of this area. A useful starting point is to use the series of tutorials provided with Windows 95 to explore the nature of operating systems. There are several options (see Figure 6) to choose from.

Windows 95 Tutorials

Choose Start

Select Help

Select one of the options

For example Using Windows

Figure 6 Windows Tutorials

This provides a useful introduction to the nature of operating systems and hence to computers but may also help learners to see their work in a different context.

Other choices are multimedia/CD-ROMs to show a range of applications and uses of ICT.

3. How can it help my children?

One approach is to introduce learners to the rich environment that educational multimedia can provide. Give them a choice of products and ask them to explore the CD-ROM to achieve a particular objective, for example:

▶ to find out about Roman Britain
▶ to take part in a quiz.

This will allow learners to begin to see one role for the computer to play in education, that is, to provide information. It also helps them to practise mouse skills since most multimedia CD-ROMs require considerable mouse use to navigate your way around them.

An alternative approach is to undertake the same type of exercise but using the Internet. However, this is difficult unless the learners are familiar with the keyboard and mouse and are not completely new to using computers.

4. Don't want to be left behind

It is probably appropriate with learners who feel that they are being left behind by the use of new technology to introduce them to some advanced applications. Only a minority of learners have had the opportunity to use the Internet so demonstrate the World Wide Web to them.

▶ Access the Internet explaining how the system works in straightforward terms:
  ● Internet service providers
  ● modem calling a central telephone number
  ● central number linked to another computer which is on the Internet
  ● World Wide Web being millions of sites.
▶ Ask them to pick a topic which interests them.
  ● Carry out a search for their topic using a search engine.
  ● Let them choose one of the identified pages and explore the site.

▶ Offer them a selection of other sites which you have already identified as interesting.

HOW TO AVOID CONFUSING THE LEARNERS

Different operating systems look very different from each other even when running the same application, so learners new to computers working on Windows 3.1 may find it very confusing to overhear an explanation of the application on Windows 95. Even observing the different screen displays may confuse learners as they will wonder why their display is different.

Learners need to have some understanding of different operating systems and applications in order to become competent independent users, but at this early stage it is potentially a source of confusion.

Ideally every computer should be identically configured. However, if this is not possible then separate the computers running different operating systems or applications and explain that there are different systems being used. It can be a useful opportunity to explain that systems do vary. Some learners will have used machines at work, or at home, which use different operating systems and applications. This will need to be explained and learners will frequently want to know if the same approach will work on their own computer or application.

If you are using computers which are used by other groups then the configuration of the application and desktop can be changed between sessions so that a learner can easily be confused. It is best to make a virtue of this possibility by explaining the versatility of modern operating systems and applications. If you do not want to introduce this sort of explanation too early in the course then you must check the system each time you use it.

In the longer term it is important that learners understand that they can transfer their understanding of one application or operating system to another product (e.g. Word to WordPerfect). Demonstrating the relationship between different applications is a key part of understanding that transfer is possible, as well as understanding how to do it. This requires learners to experience a range of products. However, at the start of a course it is sensible to keep the issues straightforward and avoid overloading the learners with too much information.

LAYOUT

It is important to arrange the room to aid learning and communication. However, in many cases the tutor has few choices but to accept a standard layout. The key is to consider how to maximise the possibilities of the room and minimise its limitations.

For example: if learners have to share a printer then it can be used as an opportunity to see each other's output and compare it with their own. This can assist communication and aid sharing of ideas and discoveries and not simply the printouts.

The main point is to structure your approach around the resources you have available. A wide range of room layouts can be effective. The two key variables are to encourage communication between learners and to maximise visibility so that a tutor can observe all the learners in order to identify those who need support. Four examples of room layouts (see figure 7) are:

1. Computer work areas follow the walls of the room so each learner has the potential of colleagues on either side to ask for help. The tutor has a clear view of all the learners' screens so is able to identify anyone who is having problems.
2. Computer work areas are arranged in rows which maximises the use of space and allows learners the potential to communicate with colleagues on either side and in front of them. However, the tutor has poor visibility of learners without walking up and down each row.
3. Computer work areas are arranged in clusters so that physical structure encourages each cluster of learners to work together. The tutor has better visibility than with the rows layout. However, there are still limitations.
4. This is a variation on example 1 with the addition of a central

table on which handouts, exercises and demonstration materials can be placed. This encourages learners to move around the room and to talk with their colleagues. Tutors' visibility should still be good.

Figure 7 Four room layouts

WORKING IN PAIRS AND INDIVIDUALLY

In many situations, providing each learner with their own computer is probably the best approach. However, sharing computers should not be rejected automatically. Working in pairs has advantages. Adults may prefer to work with a friend and can provide each other with mutual support. The limitations are that hands-on experience is reduced, and if one partner is more experienced or confident than the other there is a risk that the inexperienced or less confident person may simply observe, rather than take an active part in the session.

The tutor should observe how the pair work together and ensure it is a positive experience for both of them. It is possible to prepare exercises requiring the participation of both parties, which may help counter the negative factors.

Example

Partner Exercise

first partner should ....

second partner should now ....

first partner should ....

The exercise should be split with each person taking it in turn to carry out a part of the operation.

In most cases individuals will be working on their own with a personal computer. It is therefore important to prepare a series of exercises and activities to structure their exploration of the computer. The exercises should be developed to allow each learner to work at their own pace. This means that within a few sessions of the course starting, the learners will have diverged as some progress rapidly and others need more time to become competent.

It is important to:

▶ avoid putting anyone under pressure to work faster than the pace they are comfortable with
▶ encourage the learners to support each other
▶ review each piece of work individually with the learner as it is completed (providing group feedback is not appropriate when everyone is working on different topics and exercises).

INDIVIDUAL NEEDS

As in most education and training events preparation is the key to quality. It is important to consider and develop your approach, exercises, equipment and resources to assist learners with special needs who:

▶ are visually impaired. There are a range of systems available for learners who are visually disabled. These range from magnifying panels to speech synthesis devices which will explain to the learners what is displayed. Windows 95 provides some facilities to aid people who are visually impaired.

▶ speak English as a second language. It is possible to purchase versions of applications and operating systems in a large number of languages as well as keyboards adapted to other alphabets.

▶ are physically disabled. Ask the learner how best to support them. There are many examples of the tutor jumping to the conclusion that they have a problem when the learner does not see one. There are a wide range of devices and adaptations available to help disabled users make full use of a computer.

▶ have learning difficulties.

There are many adaptations and devices which can help, from the simple to the complex.

Examples

1. Copy holders.
2. Keyboard emulation of a mouse.
2. Concept keyboards.
3. Predictive word-processors.
4. Keyguards.
5. Voice input.
6. Trackerballs and joysticks as an alternative to mice.

Professional advice is essential before you make your decisions. A series of information sheets is available on the BECTA website which give many useful contacts who can help. Appendix 1 has a number of useful addresses which you may find helpful.

4

Confusing issues

Modern computer operating systems and applications are complex. They offer a multitude of different options and possibilities to the user so that it is not surprising that learners can be easily confused. Some of the things which confuse new learners are:

WINDOWS

▶ The changing size of windows often confuses especially if produced accidentally.

▶ Students can easily feel they have lost a file when by accident they open a second document on top of their first efforts.

▶ Unexpected messages are often a source of confusion, e.g. you cancel an operation and get messages such as 'Do you want to save?' In most cases you don't but if this happens prior to any work on saving files you are probably left confused.

▶ Learners with experience of non-windows computers may be more confused by the windows environment than new learners.

▶ Minimising, maximising, closing and re-sizing windows all require accurate use of a pointer. Re-sizing in particular requires very precise positioning of the pointer over window edge to allow the double-headed arrow to appear – the learner then has to hold the button down and drag the edge – the idea that you can drag all four edges can take a little time to absorb.

KEYBOARD SHORT CUTS

▶ Keyboard short cuts can often be accidentally operated (e.g. when using the left-hand shift key, it is easy to press the ctrl key by mistake – this key combined with a letter key often operates an unintended process.

▶ Keyboard short cuts which are intentionally used can also be difficult as new users will frequently hold down the keys for too long or repeatedly press them which causes the short cut to repeat. This often results in a series of identical windows opening or causes the same software to run several times. It is very confusing to learners.

▶ The learner who is new to typing usually looks at the keyboard and is often unaware if they have made an error or accidentally activated a short cut so are normally bewildered when they look up. This is especially troublesome when combined with accidentally moving from insert to overwrite modes within a word-processor or if cursor is wrongly positioned on the screen (e.g. within the text).

INPUT DEVICES

▶ Although learners have problems with using a mouse they also have difficulties using a keyboard. They initially find identifying keys difficult (e.g. shift key) and frequently confuse keys (e.g. backspace and enter keys) with each other. They may accidentally touch a key such as Caps Lock and then be unclear how to cancel it. The difference between backspace and delete keys is a source of puzzlement until it is explained.

▶ Input devices such as mice and touch pads are difficult to master and require practice. Windows-type environments require considerable skill and precision with mice or other input devices.

▶ A skilled mouse-user may still encounter difficulties with devices such as touch pads.

▶ Alternative ways of undertaking an action (e.g. menu item or icon) confuses learners but sometimes is helpful in allowing the tutor to make a learning point from the incident.

▶ Double- and single-clicking and dragging – clicking is relatively straightforward with the main problem being to position the pointer accurately. Double-clicking is very difficult with the principal problem being the gap between the two clicks – one-to-one demonstration is effective while a verbal explanation is insufficient.

▶ Learners frequently click on wrong items since they are often very close together and they have limited dexterity – this often leaves them unsure of what to do.

▶ Learners are often observed treating the mouse very gently and pointing it the wrong way, turning it up-side down, etc. Tutors should suggest how to hold the mouse and position fingers. One-to-one demonstration is the most effective method.

▶ Tutors often ask learners to move the mouse around the mat and to observe what follows on the screen. However, several learners will press the buttons although expressly asked not to – some of this is accidental and both left- and right-mouse buttons are pressed.

OPERATING SYSTEMS

▶ Some confusion occurs between features of operating system and application perhaps partly caused by having similar names Microsoft Windows 95 and Microsoft Office. Learners often do not see the difference between them.

▶ Experience of a different operating system can be very confusing for a learner (e.g. Windows 3.1 and Windows 95) – especially when a learner has their own computer at home running one and the computer at the centre running the other. This is probably also true of different versions of applications (e.g. Word 6 and Word 97).

TEXT

▶ Word wrap causes people who have used a typewriter some difficulties.

▶ Learners working on an exercise supplied to them by the tutor sometimes believe that the layout of words (e.g. words per line) should be identical – this encourages them to use line breaks in their text. It is important that exercises are identical to what can be achieved using the desired approach, although errors can be turned into learning points.

▶ New learners do not always realise when making a hardware change (eg. using colour printer) that it is not sufficient to make the hardware change, they need also to inform the computer that they are using different equipment.

▶ In a word-processor the cursor position and changes to the pointer shape from an arrow to an I bar needs to be carefully explained. Text appears at the cursor and the I bar can move the cursor but both are on the screen at the same time. This is potentially confusing.

SAVING

▶ Saving onto floppy disks is confusing (e.g. A and C drives, which is the right way up and how do you insert the disk into the drive?)

▶ Confusion occurs about where files have been saved to and what they are called.

▶ Learners often learn to save by rote so that they have no understanding where a file has been saved to (eg. A and C drives).

GENERAL

▶ Learners may need reassuring about what they need to remember (e.g. do I need to remember all these icons?).

▶ Computer language is new and needs to be explained (e.g. what is a font?).

▶ When demonstrating how to do something using menus, obviously other options are visible to students – they may well want to know what the other things do – either immediately or later.

▶ Files often seem to disappear to beginners and even more advanced users because the learners cannot remember the names of their files or simply because the system is only showing them files in a particular format rather than all formats.

▶ The tutor has to recognise a variety of mistakes, e.g. deleting a row of icons, opening a second or third blank document on top of the exercise. Learners will do what you least expect.

SCROLLING

▶ If a window is made smaller, a scroll bar appears which needs to be explained by the tutor.

▶ Scrolling to left and right can be confusing at first.

▶ Using START and Program to select an application is difficult for learners since it requires them to move the pointer in a straight line (within blue bar) to select the correct application. This is more than a dexterity issue since logically if you can see the application, why can't you go directly to it?

5 Next sessions

The first session should have established a sound foundation on which to build on in the forthcoming sessions. The emphasis in later sessions should still concentrate on:

- developing the learners' confidence and reducing their anxieties
- encouraging mutual assistance
- providing appropriate individual support
- avoiding confusing learners by overloading them with information
- allowing learners to work at their own pace.

Other key features of the programme of sessions should be:

REVIEW

Learners find it useful to review topics. Starting each session with a brief review of the topics covered in the last session serves to help learners to develop their understanding.

OBJECTIVES

Over the whole programme learners should develop:
- confidence

- specific understanding of a range of applications and computer systems such as:
  - Internet
  - word-processing
  - e-mail
  - databases
  - spreadsheets
  - operating systems
- into an independent learner who can transfer their knowledge and skills to new situations (e.g. new versions of applications).

OPERATING SYSTEM

An understanding of the operating system is important in developing an independent learner who can solve problems and adapt to change. This needs to integrated into each session and many exercises so that gradually a clear picture of the functions and nature of the system emerges.

Operating systems are potentially very confusing and need to be approached in a straightforward systematic way. Learners need as many opportunities as possible to practise using the operating system. It is important over the whole course to differentiate between the operating system and application software. Learners often find it very difficult to understand the difference between them.

APPLICATIONS

There are a wide range of possible applications to include in an ICT programme. Learners often have clear ideas about what they would like to use. These are frequently linked to their original reasons for attending the course. The main options are word-processing, painting and drawing, spreadsheets, e-mail, the Internet, desktop publishing and databases. Although many courses begin with word-processing there is no particular reason not to

start with other applications. A sound approach is based on:
- individual achievement – give the learners the option of developing items they would like (e.g. own accounts, business cards, letter headings, standard letters and searching for information on the Internet)
- practical exercises
- mutual support.

METHODS

The emphasis on practical individual work is good practice in most cases. However, this should not preclude the use of other approaches such as:
- short presentations to the whole class
- group and individual demonstrations
- discussions
- open and computer-based learning
- reviews and summaries.

CLIMATE

It is important to establish a climate of exploration and experiential learning. Computer systems are complex environments and learners need to recognise that they will frequently discover new items which they need to try out. The spirit of 'having a go' is important. Learners need to believe that they can learn from their mistakes and that this is the accepted way of working with computers.

SUPPORT

The support of learners is important in all sessions. Learners often comment that waiting for help was the major factor in their dropping out of courses. In a class of 12 the tutor is likely to be asked constantly to answer questions, solve problems and sort out technical difficulties. With groups larger than 12 the waiting time is likely to be excessive.

SUMMARIES

At the end of relevant sections of work, or each session, try to provide summaries of the key points and important issues covered. New users often find differentiating between important and trivial points difficult because they lack an overall context for the information.

6 Some suggestions

Some suggestions are now provided for covering word-processing, spreadsheets, databases, the Internet, e-mail and painting and drawing in an information and communication technology learning programme. In many cases applications can be effectively introduced by taking the group through a guided tour of them to identify key elements. This can be achieved individually, through small group demonstration or by a whole-class demonstration using a video projector or LCD panel to allow everyone to see the screen.

Learners often find that examples of professional outcomes of applications are interesting and helpful to themselves in realising their potential use. Try to provide a range of examples such as CD-ROM databases, letters, publications and accounts which they can see.

WORD-PROCESSING

Frequently, you will find skilled typists in a group of new computer users. In contrast other learners will have never touched a keyboard. This needs to be allowed for when developing exercises. An experienced typist will quickly enter many paragraphs of text while a new user will be entering a couple of sentences. Unless the course requires the development of typing speeds do not make the course a test of entering text.

The basic points to cover are:

- locating and loading the word-processor (e.g. double-clicking on icon or locating program through Start and Program menu)
- keyboard layout (e.g. compare with typewriter for the typists present)
- exploring the application to identify the main features of menus and toolbars
- using practical exercises involving the input of a text passage, in order to allow learners the opportunity to use and explore some of the following (to cover all of them will take several sessions):
  - word wrap
  - backspace and delete key
  - copy and paste functions
  - cut and paste function
  - ins key (insert or overwrite functions)
  - margins
  - justification (align: left, right, centre and full)
  - line spacing
  - bold, italics and underline
  - fonts and font sizes
  - undo
  - spell check
  - find and replace
  - go to
  - headers and footers
  - toolbars
  - borders
  - bullets
  - zoom control
  - page numbering
  - paragraph numbering
  - tables
  - columns
  - inserting clipart
- saving the text entered as a file on either a floppy disk, hard disk or network server

▶ practising using Save As function to change name or location of a file

▶ loading text saved on a floppy disk, hard disk or network server

▶ printing the text files to show the learners what they have achieved and give the printouts to them to take away.

SPREADSHEETS

Spreadsheets are an important application for the learners who are seeking to develop computer skills to improve their employment opportunities. The key points to cover are:

▶ what is a spreadsheet?

▶ locating and loading the spreadsheet (e.g. double-clicking on icon or locating program through Start and Program menu)

▶ exploring the application to identify main features of menu and toolbars

▶ loading/creating a spreadsheet file to:
  ● add rows and columns
  ● add data as numbers, text and formulae
  ● format cells – size, decimal points, currency, etc
  ● adjust column width
  ● format rows and columns
  ● replication
  ● sorting data
  ● basic functions of spreadsheets
  ● creating a header and footer

▶ explaining the changing shape of the mouse pointer

▶ saving the data entered as a file on either a floppy disk or hard disk

▶ printing the spreadsheet file

There are other more advanced spreadsheet functions which should only be included if the group is particularly interested in spreadsheets.

Ensure that these other spreadsheet functions are covered following the same approach of using exercises. Items to include are:

▶ working with more than one spreadsheet
▶ producing graphs and charts
▶ using integrated software

DATABASES

People come into contact with databases many times during their lives. Every time they contact the utility companies, their bank or building society someone looks up their details on a database and then updates the record. Most people are unaware that they have been in contact with a database. The design and development of a database requires significant computer skills and understanding. During a basic ICT course it is unlikely that time will be available to develop a new database except in a small-scale partial way (e.g. by simulating a database using a spreadsheet). However, it is important to develop a clear understanding of the nature of modern relational databases because of their widespread use in society.

This course should provide a practical introduction to:

▶ what is a database?
▶ locating and loading a database (e.g. double-clicking on icon or locating program through Start and Program menu)
▶ loading/using an existing database to:
  ● sort data
  ● search data
  ● select data
  ● present data on the screen
  ● use Help functions
▶ saving the contents as a file on either a floppy disk or hard disk
▶ printing the contents.

Database packages such as Microsoft Access 97 provide example databases which can be used instead of developing a new database, and have database wizards which allow the process of creating a database to be simplified. By a careful combination of such features it is possible to provide rich experience of the application without spending excessive amounts of time.

INTERNET

A relatively small proportion of the population has used the Internet and most people are curious about what it is and how it works. It is good practice to provide explanations of the different components which make up the Internet so that learners gain an understanding of the whole context of the system. This can be introduced in a series of short talks followed by practical sessions. The main points to cover are:

▶ what is the Internet and the World Wide Web?
▶ how do you access the Internet? What do you need?
▶ exploring a browser
▶ accessing a website (provide the learners with a choice of sites)
▶ exploring a website (e.g. links, move forward and back through the site)
▶ printing pages from sites, saving pages as html files and downloading files
▶ undertaking exercises based on finding information, surfing the web and investigating World Wide Web
▶ using a range of search engines
▶ exploring other browser or WWW site functions such as:
  ● bookmarks
  ● favourites
  ● newsgroups
  ● history
  ● chat lines

E-MAIL

Many people have used e-mail as part of their work. However, the majority of the adult population has probably never used or seen e-mail. People often quickly recognise the power of e-mail and rapidly learn how to use it. The main points to cover are:

▶ what is e-mail?
▶ how does e-mail and the Internet relate to each other?
▶ exploring the e-mail system by sending messages to each other
▶ receiving e-mail
▶ replying to a message.

Exercises should be used to investigate the following features of the system:

▶ headers (e.g. address, multiple copies, etc.)
▶ subject
▶ main body of text (this provides an additional opportunity for the learner to practise text editing)
▶ inbox
▶ outbox
▶ forwarding mail
▶ attachments
▶ address books
▶ mail groups.

PAINTING AND DRAWING

Individual ability to draw varies but by using a computer application almost everyone can provide an acceptable image. For many beginners using a Paint package is both enjoyable and motivating. They can see the computer providing the means to allow them to achieve a goal which normally they would not attempt.

Painting requires good mouse control, so this can be combined with exercises to develop mouse skills of accuracy, clicking and dragging objects. In many courses introducing Painting applications in an early session can be good practice especially if you need to concentrate on the mouse.

The key issues to cover are:

▶ what is a painting and drawing application?
▶ locating and loading the drawing programme (e.g. double-clicking on icon or locating program through Start and Program menu)
▶ loading clipart in order to:
  ● copy and resize clipart
  ● modify image
▶ creating an image with a mouse in freehand
  ● draw boxes, circles, text and lines
  ● use colour, shading and borders
▶ saving the image as a file on either a floppy disk or hard disk
▶ printing the image.

GENERAL SYSTEM AREAS

Some general areas which learners should cover:

▶ start and shut down the computer
▶ create a directory (folder) and a sub-directory (understand the directory/folder structure)
▶ move and copy files
▶ delete files (single and groups of files)
▶ create a file
▶ naming and renaming files
▶ use of wild cards
▶ examine a directory and understand information (size of files, date created, etc.)
▶ format a floppy disk
▶ write protect disks and files
▶ backup files
▶ save files on a floppy and hard disk

➤ save as function
➤ virus and anti-virus measures
➤ select printers
➤ print a file on a printer.

Many of these suggestions require significant amounts of time to achieve so their inclusion will depend on the length and purpose of the course.

7
Teaching techniques and tutors

A whole range of techniques is available to the tutor and it is good practice to employ a mixture of appropriate methods. This will ensure to some extent that individuals with different learning styles are not disadvantaged. Some of the key approaches which should be considered are:

SPEED

It is important to pace each session to suit the needs of the group of learners. Emphasise from the beginning of the programme that everyone can work at their own speed. Learners who have access to computers outside of the sessions are likely to work faster than others. Don't expect everyone to maintain the same rate of progress. Some key points are:

▶ Be careful not to overload people with information. Present each new item as a meaningful chunk. However, do not slow individuals down.
▶ Recap important information at intervals
▶ Present information using different methods (e.g. orally, in handouts, exercises and visually).
▶ Relate new information to existing knowledge (e.g. provide a context, use analogies and examples).
▶ Encourage questions and reflection on each new chunk of information.

▶ Encourage everyone to take regular breaks.
▶ Balance new information with practice in applying it and developing skills.
▶ Allow each person to choose when they want to move onto the next step.
▶ Remove the stress from the room and encourage an attitude of trying again.

WHOLE-CLASS TEACHING

Whole group activities are an effective and efficient way of introducing or reviewing a subject provided you do not overdo it. A short talk (10 to 20 minutes) or demonstration will hold the attention of your learners providing you take action to reduce the distraction of computer displays. There is little alternative to asking everyone to switch off monitors and to face you. It is very difficult to gain the attention of a group who have been using equipment. They are concentrating on their exercises and not on you. It is therefore worth considering the timing of whole-class teaching. Good times to employ whole class methods are:

▶ start of session
▶ after a break
▶ finish of session.

By using an LCD panel or a video/data projector it is possible to demonstrate to the whole class how to use applications. It is very effective if combined with asking the learners to work with you and to follow the demonstration on their own machines. A suggested sequence could be:

▶ show them the whole sequence of steps so that they understand the whole operation
▶ repeat the process step-by-step explaining what is happening
▶ ask them to follow you on their own machines as you work through it again.

However, the normal rules of using any visual aid apply (e.g. make sure everyone can see).

DEMONSTRATION

Demonstrating is a very useful approach to teaching the practical skills and techniques of ICT. A key factor is visibility. If you are showing a learner how to hold a mouse it is likely that only one or two people can see the details well enough for it to be effective. With demonstrating the use of an application probably only two or three learners will be able to see all the steps on a monitor clearly. A common sight is the tutor kneeling on the floor beside the computer in an effort to avoid blocking the learners' view of the display. It is a false economy to pack people around a display. Many will be unable to see what is going on and the danger is that they will feel restrained in telling you that they cannot see.

Demonstrations can take two main forms in a computer class:

▶ watch me do this
▶ do this with me.

In both cases it is important to:

▶ clearly tell everyone watching what it is about, for example:
  ● this is double-clicking
▶ gain the learners' attention by explaining why it is important, for example:
  ● double-clicking is the way you start a programme
▶ break complex tasks down into meaningful chunks and show how they link together, for example:
  ● single-click on Start to open up a window
  ● place your pointer over Program so that it highlights and a list of programs will appear
  ● place your pointer over Accessories so that it highlights and a list of programs appears

- click on Paint and the program will load (Paint Window will open)

If you carry out this example at your normal speed then most if not all your learners will miss at least one step. Demonstrate the sequence of operations one at a time and then link them together. The display provides you with a useful visual aid in that at each step you can release the mouse and the display will show the steps taken. Figure 8 shows an example of the display.

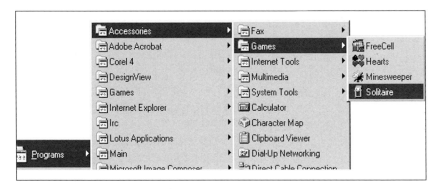

Figure 8 Using the display as a visual aid

▶ ensure that the learners practise the skill immediately after you have finished

▶ encourage the learners to help each other – they are more likely to ask each other questions than you

▶ check comprehension by walking around the room observing progress and giving help as required.

SMALL GROUP LEARNING

Working in small groups is highly effective in that learners often feel more able to ask questions and make comments. The limitation is often the size of the screen; frequently ICT group work involves using the computer and everyone must be able to see the display in order to contribute. In practical terms a group is probably limited to no more than three individuals. However, you can change the membership of the groups and thus aid whole-group communication.

INDIVIDUAL LEARNING

The major learning method is likely to involve individual learners working on their own. ICT requires the individual to develop personal knowledge and skill and this will require a great deal of individual effort. In order to make progress, support for the individual learner is crucial. Tutors will normally move continuously around the room to make themselves available and to diagnose if someone is likely to need help. Supporting a class of 12 new users is a demanding and often exhausting task and ideally volunteers or other staff should be available to provide extra support to the group.

New learners who are regularly left without assistance for even short periods can easily become discouraged. Their confidence is reduced and the seeds for dropping out can be sown. To avoid this situation ensure that support in the form of the tutor, volunteer helpers or other learners is always available.

COMPUTER-BASED LEARNING

There are two CD-ROMs which have been produced to provide the initial experience of using information technology. They are:

▶ Computers Don't Bite by the BBC
▶ IT for All programme by Department of Trade and Industry

There are also a large number of computer-based tutorials related to information technology subjects. Many of them are focused on particular applications such as Word 6 or Windows 95. However, they can make a useful contribution when you need to concentrate on an application. Computer-based learning offers:

- individual support
- learning at your own pace
- clear objectives.

By providing the learners with a computer-based learning (CBL) package, it limits them to a defined area, ensures they practise a set of defined tasks and develop a set of prescribed skills. However, it reduces opportunities to learn from their own mistakes and exploration, which are powerful methods in developing ICT skills. This may frustrate more advanced learners. The tutor needs to be familiar with the tutorial so that she or he can incorporate it into the course of study at the right moment and know when it is suitable for individual use.

Frequently, computer-based learning is designed to be used with a minimum of support so that it can help to reduce the burden on tutors and allow for larger group sizes. However, the tutor should not assume that their learners will not need support. The ability to use computer-based learning assumes some degree of skill. Often, packages assume a reasonable level of mouse dexterity or keyboard skills which may limit their use with new learners.

PAPER-BASED OPEN LEARNING

There is a wide range of open learning materials available related to ICT skills and knowledge. Open learning is useful in that it allows tutors to support larger groups of learners than they could conventionally while letting the learners work at their own speed. However, designing learning materials which cover every eventuality is difficult and beginners can easily become confused if support is not immediately available. Learners will often react to a problem by trying something if help does not arrive quickly. This may solve the problem but it also has the potential to further change the display so that it is outside the scope of the workbook. Workbooks are probably more suitable to learners who have achieved a basic understanding of information technology (e.g. familiarity with the basics of the operating system).

FEEDBACK

Both learners and tutors need feedback. Learners need to know how they are doing and tutors need to assess if their approach is effective. There are many opportunities for both types of feedback during a course. Some of them are:

- on completion of an exercise
- reviewing the last session at the start of the next
- reviewing a topic
- checking individual progress
- introducing a new topic
- inviting questions at all times
- feedback sheets at the end of a programme.

QUESTIONS

Questions are a useful way of checking on the learners' understanding. However, take care not to interrogate them and be receptive to their questions to you. These will also help you to gain an insight into how your learners' understanding is developing.

The key to asking a good question is patience. You must allow learners enough time to answer. Some tutors expect an almost instant response. A few moments' delay will allow learners to reflect and to give you an informed answer. If a student is unable to answer then rephrase your question or ask them if there is a problem.

It is vital to encourage your learners to ask you questions. This helps to ensure that the session is meeting their needs. Questions provide you with an effective way of checking understanding both when you ask questions and answer them.

COACHING

Good coaches have great patience with their learners. They treat each person as an individual with a unique set of abilities, knowledge and understanding. Good coaches:

▶ have fun with their learners
▶ agree realistic objectives with their learners
▶ fit their approach to learners' ability and preferred learning style
▶ plan constructive practice
▶ break tasks into straightforward meaningful chunks
▶ emphasise success and praise achievement.

PRACTICE

Practice is critical to the successful understanding and use of ICT. If possible, it is very useful to allow learners to have access to computers and appropriate applications between sessions. Many learners find that a week between opportunities to practise their new skills leaves them vulnerable to losing some understanding. During a course it soon becomes apparent which students are able to practise between sessions since they will often make rapid progress. Learners who rely solely on the course are likely to make slower progress and may even find it difficult to remember what they covered the previous session.

It is therefore important to allow each learner to work at his or her own pace but also to develop approaches which will help both groups of learners. For example:

▶ regular reviews to aid memory
▶ exercises to take away to structure practice.

HANDOUTS

Handouts are a useful means of summarising topics and providing learners with notes of the main issues covered. They can take many forms and serve a range of functions such as:

- summary of a topic
- provide space for learners to add their own notes
- linking handouts to exercises
- providing electronic handouts (i.e. Lotus ScreenCam Movies).

8 Roles

TUTOR

For the new computer users there is probably no more important person than their tutor. Most adults are not confident about their ability to learn to use ICT equipment and applications. The tutor has a key role in developing their confidence. This requires considerable skills and understanding of ICT, learning and communicating.

It is a demanding task. Supporting what may seem a small group of 12 learners is often exhausting and stretching. A tutor must be able to diagnose the many small and different problems which learners exploring complex modern computer products find themselves in. Learners must be encouraged to work things out for themselves but not allowed to become confused or discouraged.

VOLUNTEERS

Volunteers are a valuable resource in the ICT classroom. They can provide additional one-to-one support, technical help and ensure no learner is left without assistance for too long. The combination of tutor and volunteer is very effective if they work as a team providing mutual support. In order for this to happen each must be clear about their role.

Volunteers can play many roles within the ICT classroom. However, their role must be compatible with the tutor and both need to form a team. It is therefore important to agree roles.

Some examples are:

1. Volunteers have a designated caseload of learners whom they provide with one-to-one support.
2. Volunteers and tutor observe learners together with the aim of identifying those with problems and offering appropriate help.
3. Volunteers undertake specific teaching tasks often related to their individual expertise (e.g. demonstrations of the Internet).

Volunteers need teaching, coaching, mentoring and training skills. It is not sufficient that they are expert computer users.

TECHNICAL SUPPORT

Apart from the key resource of a tutor it is important to have access to technical support. Computers, printers and other equipment need to be maintained and they do breakdown. The roles of tutor and technical support are normally separate but it may be possible to combine them. Learners frequently have problems telling the two roles apart and it may be useful to consider multi-skilling. That is giving the tutor some basic technical skills and the technical support some coaching/instructor skills similar to the volunteers.

TRAINING OF TUTORS AND VOLUNTEERS

ICT is subject to continuous change so tutors need to have opportunities to develop themselves. Some simple steps are:

▶ provide access to new versions of applications before introducing them to the course
▶ ensure tutors have the opportunity to meet and discuss approaches with other tutors
▶ personal development plans.

9 Some advice for a successful IT education and training event

A successful ICT event or course needs to provide an environment which:

▶ supports learners
▶ develops confidence
▶ creates a climate of experiment, exploration and experiential learning
▶ provides an active and motivating experience which maximises individual choice and encourages them to return for more
▶ encourages mutual support
▶ provides individual feedback
▶ seeks feedback to allow for continuous improvement.

Appendix 1
Useful organisations

Associations/Agencies

Basic Skills Agency (formerly ALBSU)
Commonwealth House
1–19 New Oxford Street
London WC1A 1NU

BECTA, http://www.becta.org.uk

British Computer Society (BCS)
  Disabled Specialist Group
Geoff Busby, BCS, GEC
Marconi Research Centre,
West Hanningfield Road,
Great Baddow, Chelmsford
Essex CM2 8HN

British Institute of Learning
  Disabilities (BILD)
Wolverhampton Road
Kidderminster
Worcestershire DY10 3PP

Centre for Micro-Assisted
  Communication (CENMAC)
Eltham Green Complex, 4th Floor
1a Middle Park Avenue
Eltham, London SE9 5HL

Foundation for Communication for
  the Disabled
25 High Street
Woking
Surrey GU21 1BW
Tel: 01483 727848
Fax: 01483 771109

National Federation of ACCESS
  Centres
Hereward College of FE
Bramston Crescent
Tile Hill Lane
Coventry
West Midlands
CV4 9SW

Royal National Institute for the
  Blind
224 Great Portland Street,
London
W1N 6AA

Royal National Institute for Deaf
  People
19-23 Featherstone Street
London
EC1Y 8SL

Scottish Council for Educational
   Technology
74 Victoria Crescent Road
Glasgow G12 9JN

The CALL Centre
4 Buccleugh Place
Edinburgh
EH8 9LW

Special Educational Needs Joint
   Initiative for Training (SENJIT)
University of London
Institute of Education
20 Bedford Way
London WC1H OAL
Tel: 0171 612 6273/4
Fax: 0171 612 6304

Disability Information Systems in
   Higher Education
Department of Applied Computing
University of Dundee
Dundee
DD1 4HN
enquiries@disinhe.ac.uk

Communication aids

Ability Net
Hassel House,
Link Industrial Estate,
Malvern,
Worcs WR14 1UQ

ACE Centre
Broadbent Road
Watersheddings
Oldham OL1 4HU

ACE Centre
Ormerod School
Waynette Road
Headington
Oxford OX3 8DD

Belfast Communication Advice
   Centre
RDF Building
Musgrove Park Hospital
Stockmans lane
Belfast
BT9 7JB

Equipment suppliers

Alpha Vision Ltd
North Estate
Podington
High Wycombe
Bucks
HP14 3BE

Cambridge Adaptive
   Communications
The Mount
Toft
Cambridge CB3 7RL

Dolphin Systems for People with
   Disabilities
PO Box 83
Worcester
WR3 8TU

Foundation for Communication for
   the Disabled
25 High Street
Woking
Surrey
GU21 1BW

IBM UK Ltd
National Enquiry Centre
PO Box 41
North harbour
Portsmouth
Hampshire PO6 3AU

Techno-Vision Systems Ltd
76 Bunting Road Industrial Estate
Northampton
NN2 6EE

IT awareness raising

The Computers Don't Bite Office
BBC
Room 2319
White City
201 Wood Lane
London W12 7TS

IT for All
Department of Trade and Industry
151 Buckingham Palace Road
London
SW1W 9SS

Open learning

British Association for Open
    Learning (BAOL)
Suite 16 Pixmore House
Pixmore Avenue
Letchworth
Hertfordshire
SG6 1JG

Qualifications

The British Computer Society
1 Sanford Street
Swindon
Wiltshire SN1 1HJ

University of Cambridge
Local Examinations Syndicate
1 Hills Road
Cambridge
CB1 2EU

City and Guilds of London Institute
1 Giltspur Street
London EC1A 9DD

National Open College Network
University of Derby
Kedleston
Derby DE22 1GB

RSA Examinations Board
Westwood Way
Coventry CV4 8HS

Technology-based training

Technologies for Training
c/o Guildford Educational Services
32 Castle Street
Guildford
Surrey GU1 3UW

References and further reading

BBC (1997), *Computers Don't Bite Campaign Report*, BBC Education

Bissland, V 1997, *Easy for Some: Attitudes of learning in later Life students to Learning Computer Skills*, Senior Studies Institute, University of Strathclyde

Clarke, A (1998), *IT Awareness Raising for Adults*, Department for Education and Employment, OL254

Clarke, A (1999), *Computing for Adults*, Hodder and Stoughton

European Commission, *How to benefit from the Information Society* EC DG XIII Telecommunications, Information Market and Exploitation of Research

GHK Economics and Management (1998), *IT Labour Market Assessment: A Review of Available Information*, Department for Education and Employment, Research Report RR71

HMSO (1992), *Health and Safety (Display Screen Equipment Regulations)*, HMSO

HSE (1998), *Working with VDUs: Revised Edition 1998*, Health and Safety Executive

ISI (1996), *Read all about IT: A survey of public awareness of, attitudes towards, and access to Information and Communication Technologies*, IT for All, Department of Trade and Industry

Leigh, D (1991), *A Practical Approach to Group Training*, Practical Training Series, Institute for Training and Development, Kogan Page

Lockett, B (1998), *Learning styles: into the future*, Further Education Development Agency

McKeowen, S (1998), *Supporting the learner: introducing ILT issues and teaching strategies to meet individual needs*, Further Education Development Agency

NEC (1998), *Fit for CLAIT: Computer based learning material*, National Extension College

NOP 1997, *State of the Nation Research Findings: An in-depth look at Britain's attitudes towards technology*, Microsoft

Rowntree, D (1992), *Exploring Open and Distance Learning*, The Open University

Rowntree, D (1990), *Teaching Through Self-Instruction: How to Develop Open Learning materials*, Kogan Page

Sargant, N, Field, J, Francis, H, Schuller, T and Tuckett, A (1997), *The Learning Divide: A study of participation in adult learning in the United Kingdom*, National Institute of Adult Continuing Education

Siddons, S (1997), *Delivering Training*, Institute of Personnel and Development

Sutcliffe, J and Jacobsen, Y (1998), *All things being equal?*, National Institute of Adult Continuing Education

Wolverhampton University (1996), *tecknowledgeable: Staff development in enabling and adaptive technologies for students with disabilities*, University of Wolverhampton